TURNER

TURNER

New & Selected Poems

David Dabydeen

CAPE POETRY

First published 1994

1 3 5 7 9 10 8 6 4 2

© David Dabydeen 1994

David Dabydeen has asserted his right under the
Copyright, Designs and Patents Act, 1988
to be identified as the author of this work

First published in the United Kingdom in 1994 by
Jonathan Cape
Random House, 20 Vauxhall Bridge Road, London SW1V 2SA

Random House Australia (Pty) Limited
20 Alfred Street, Milsons Point, Sydney,
New South Wales 2061, Australia

Random House New Zealand Limited
18 Poland Road, Glenfield,
Auckland 10, New Zealand

Random House South Africa (Pty) Limited
PO Box 337, Bergvlei, South Africa

Random House UK Limited Reg. No. 954009

A CIP catalogue record for this book
is available from the British Library

ISBN 0 224 03895 8

Typeset in Bembo by
SX Composing Ltd, Rayleigh, Essex
Printed and bound in Great Britain
by Mackays of Chatham PLC

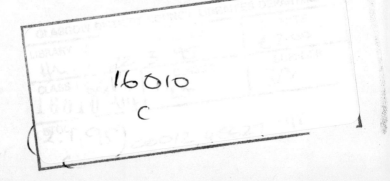

FOR MY MOTHER, VERONICA PRASAD

CONTENTS

ACKNOWLEDGEMENTS

I am grateful to Marjorie Davies for typing manuscripts; to the late Jack Lindsay for his previous kindness and his book on Turner; to Joe Harte and Anna Rutherford for their enduring friendship; and above all to Michelle Remblance for her uncanny feeling for imagery and rhythm, and the care with which she helped shape 'Turner'.

Sections from 'Turner' have appeared in *Callaloo* and *Poetry Review*.

The paintings by J. M. W. Turner are reproduced by permission:
pp. xii–xiii and p. 13 (detail): *Slave Ship (Slavers Throwing Overboard the Dead and Dying, Typhoon Coming On*, 1840, oil on canvas, Museum of Fine Arts, Boston (Henry Lillie Pierce Fund); p. 7: *A Fire at Sea* (detail), *c.* 1835, oil on canvas, Turner Collection/Tate Gallery, London; p. 19: *The Parting of Hero and Leander* (detail), 1837, oil on canvas, the Trustees of the National Gallery, London; p. 24: *Chevening Park, c.* 1801, oil (perhaps with watercolour) on paper, Turner Collection/ Tate Gallery, London; p. 25: *Sketch of a Pheasant, c.* 1815, watercolour, Ashmolean Museum, Oxford (Ruskin School Collection)

PREFACE

I

In 1840 J. M. W. Turner exhibited at the Royal Academy his finest painting in the sublime style, 'Slavers Throwing Overboard the Dead and Dying' (commonly known as 'Slave Ship'). It was not unusual for ship captains to order the drowning of sick slaves (who would fetch a low price on landing in the Caribbean), and to claim their insurance value on the basis of goods lost at sea.

Ruskin thought that 'Slave Ship' represented 'the noblest sea that Turner ever painted . . . the noblest certainly ever painted by man'. He wrote a detailed account of the composition of the painting, dwelling on the genius with which Turner illuminated sea and sky in an intense and lurid splendour of colours. 'If I were to rest Turner's immortality upon any single work, I should choose this.' (He did, by buying the painting.) Its subject, the shackling and drowning of Africans, was relegated to a brief footnote in Ruskin's essay. The footnote reads like an afterthought, something tossed overboard.

II

My poem focuses on the submerged head of the African in the foreground of Turner's painting. It has been drowned in Turner's (and other artists') sea for centuries. When it awakens it can only partially recall the sources of its life, so it invents a body, a biography, and peoples an imagined landscape. Most of the names of birds, animals and fruit are made up. Ultimately, however, the African rejects the fabrication of an idyllic past. His real desire is to begin anew in the sea but he is too trapped by grievous memory to escape history. Although the sea has transformed him – bleached him of colour and complicated his sense of gender – he still recognises himself as 'nigger'. The desire for transfiguration or newness or creative amnesia is frustrated. The agent of self-recognition is a stillborn child tossed overboard from a future ship. The child floats towards him. He wants to give it life, to mother it, but the child – his unconscious and his origin – cannot bear the future and its inventions, drowned as it is in memory of ancient cruelty. Neither can escape Turner's representation of them as exotic and sublime victims. Neither can describe themselves anew but are indelibly stained by Turner's language and imagery.

The intensity of Turner's painting is such that I believe the artist in private must have savoured the sadism he publicly denounced. I make Turner the captain of the slave ship (the stillborn child is also named Turner). Turner's well-chronicled love of children is seen in another light, as is his extreme prudence with money.

The rest of the poems in this collection are taken from my previous volumes, *Slave Song* (1984) and *Coolie Odyssey* (1988).

TURNER

I

Stillborn from all the signs. First a woman sobs
Above the creak of timbers and the cleaving
Of the sea, sobs from the depths of true
Hurt and grief, as you will never hear
But from woman giving birth, belly
Blown and flapping loose and torn like sails,
Rough sailors' hands jerking and tugging
At ropes of veins, to no avail. Blood vessels
Burst asunder, all below-deck are drowned.
Afterwards, stillness, but for the murmuring
Of women. The ship, anchored in compassion
And for profit's sake (what well-bred captain
Can resist the call of his helpless
Concubine, or the prospect of a natural
Increase in cargo?), sets sail again,
The part-born, sometimes with its mother,
Tossed overboard. Such was my bounty
Delivered so unexpectedly that at first
I could not believe this miracle of fate,
This longed-for gift of motherhood.
What was deemed mere food for sharks will become
My fable. I named it Turner
As I have given fresh names to birds and fish
And humankind, all things living but unknown,
Dimly recalled, or dead.

It plopped into the water and soon swelled
Like a brumplak seed that bursts buckshot
From its pod, falling into the pond
In the backdam of my mother's house, and fattening,
Where small boys like I was hold sticks to the water
For fish; branches stripped and shaped from the impala
Tree, no other, for we know – only the gods
Can tell how – that they bend so supple,
Almost a circle without snapping, yet strong
Enough to pull in a baby alligator.
Maybe by instinct, maybe the wisdom
Of our village elders passed down forever
(Until Turner came) which we suck in from birth
Like wood-smoke in my mother's kitchen,
Coconut shells stoking up a fire,
And I squat with my two sisters, small we are,
I don't know exactly how much in age –
Though since Turner's days I have learnt to count,
Weigh, measure, abstract, rationalise –
But we are small enough nearly to pass
Upright under the belly of the cow
Whilst our father pulls the teats and wheezes
Milk into a pakreet shell, swoosh, swoosh
Swoosh, the sound still haunts, survives the roar
And crash and endless wash and lap
Of waves, and we stoop under the belly
Of the cow and I can see I am just
Taller than its haunches, and when my sisters
Kneel their heads reach its knees. We play
Games as our father milks, crawling under
The belly like warriors, then springing up
At the other side to hurl spears at enemies
Hiding behind the chaltee tree in the cow-pen,

From which we pick twigs each morning, chew the
    ends,
Brush our teeth clean. The cow moves its head
To one side, watches us with covetous eyes
As if it wants to play, but my father
Will forbid it, for even when the milking is done,
He will not let us jump on the cow's back,
Nor decorate its heels with the blue and yellow
Bark of hemlik, nor put a chaktee straw
Into its nostrils until it sneezes
And snorts with laughter, but will lead it
Straight to pasture, and send us off to school,
To Manu, the magician, who will teach
Us how to squeeze, drain, blend, boil the juices
Of herbs for medicines, or bandage the sprained
Foot of a chicken. So the cow stands still,
But looks at us with a harlot's eye and winks,
And we can see the mischief in its face
Which our father can't because he's so far
Behind, concentrating on his fingers as if
Worshipping the gods, and it flicks its tail,
Beating off flies, but really to join in,
To lash and surprise us as we wait in ambush
Under its belly for the English
To come from another village, who will plunder
The crops, burn the huts, stampede the goats,
Drag girls away by ropes.

I dream to be small again, even though
My mother caught me with my fingers
In a panoose jar, and whilst I licked them clean
And reached for more, she came upon me,
Put one load of licks with a tamarind
Stick on my back, boxed my ears; the jar fell,
Broke, panoose dripped thickly to the floor.
Ants appeared cautiously, marched with tongues
Hanging out, like a gang of slavers;
Even though I cut myself on a sharp stone
Plunging headlong into the pond, feet splayed,
Hands folded at my chest like a straplee monkey
Diving from a branch into water, swimming
About, climbing again for another go.
I sit in the savannah minding cows,
Watching it climb and plunge all day. When I strip,
Mount the tree and dive I hit my head
On a stone waiting at the bottom of the pond.
I come up dazed, I float half-dead, I bleed
For days afterwards, for even Manu cannot
Stem the flow with his poultices soaked
In goat-dung mixed with the skin of abara fruit,
The smell of which makes me retch. My mother
Watches over me, eyes big like our cow's
But full of sadness. My sisters laugh at me,
They steal my toys and play with them, knowing
I am too weak to complain. When I awake
The house I built from barak shells, painted
With the green juice of a siddam, is in shambles,
Stilts fallen off, big holes in the roof
Where they poked their clumsy fingers in.

Girls are stupid, they know only how to wash
And cook, my father will marry them off
Soon, two goats each for bride-price. That will teach
Them not to tamper with my things and thieve.

It plopped into the water from a passing ship
Like a lime-seed spat from the scurvied mouth
Of a sailor, shooting out between
A gap in his teeth, a cannonball
From the square hole at the side of the ship
That makes me duck below the water in fright
As it booms and breaks against another's mast.
All day they spit fire to each other
Like lovers, like Sensu courting Zain
Rolling out her long red tongue whilst he
Sits sternly and cross-legged, refusing
To surrender (clay statues in the hearth
In the front-room of my father's house where
Dawntime he prayed earnestly, fed them,
Washed his fingers in a sacred bowl
Repeatedly, his tongue, his face; smeared
His forehead with green dye. When he departed
To the savannah, my sisters and me,
Awakened, hungry, our mother still lighting
The fireside and peeling yams, stole
Some of the food, nibbling sinfully
At the sweetballs of ocho and sarabell)
For if the fire of her tongue should play
Upon his body and he should melt,
The earth would tumble uncontrollably,
People spew off the edges, clutching roots
Like they do now at each other, as one ship sinks.
For days afterwards the sea is strewn with
    companions:
The gods have taken revenge on all of us.
We float together for days before the waves
Divide us. I have known them all, briefly,
I have always known them, year after year

From different sunken ships. Turner are the ones
With golden hair. His blue eyes smile at children
As he gives us sweets and a ladle from a barrel
Of shada juice. Five of us hold his hand,
Each takes a finger, like jenti cubs
Clinging to their mother's teats, as he leads us
To the ship. Why is my mother screaming
Like a harch, and where is my father?
Why does Turner forbid her to touch us
Before we board? Why are all the elders in chains?
All the fair men are Turner, I can tell
Even when sea-quats have swallowed their eyes,
Dug holes in their faces to lay their eggs.
I can tell from the silver buckles
On the black leather boots which he lets us
Polish, till we can see our faces.
Each day boys scramble at his feet, fighting
To clean them first. He promises that the most
Faithful will be given them when we land.
Only the silver survives the sea and all
Its creatures, his most faithful possession.
Even the sharks crack their teeth against it.

The women are less familiar
But I name them Adra, Zentu, Danjera,
The names of my mother and my father's wives.
They are not so ample as our women
Though the sea bloats them, the salt hardens
On their skin, a crust of white that hides
Lines of neglect, indelicacies. The sea prepares
Their festive masks, salt crystals like a myriad
Of sequins hemmed into their flesh through golden
Threads of hair. The sea decorates, violates.
Limbs break off, crabs roost between their breasts
Feeding. The sea strips them clean. I am ashamed
To look upon the nakedness of my mothers.

When Turner came he brought none of his women.
I have only known them abroad, startled
At their first appearance, after a storm, ship
Toppled in an instant, spilling creatures
With long hair and slender waists. I gazed
Upon the fineness of their lips which the sea
Soon puffed and burst. Paler than their men,
Miniature, their hands barely the size
Of a chintoo leaf, just as softly creased.
These were not hands to rattle padlock and chain,
They would sooner beguile knots, melt iron
With a touch, loosen the greed anchored
In men's hearts.

I had forgotten the years, now wakened
By the creature that washed towards me.
Yet another ship passed, familiar sails stretched
Upon racks of wind, ropes taut against spars,
Enough to rip a man's hand trapped there,
Careless with rum, wistful for a shore
Of women. None of these things disturbed me
Then, not the commandments of braided
Officers, nor the sobbing of offenders
Tied naked to the mast, cold winds like gannets
Gathering at their flesh. For years I had known
These scenes, and I had forgotten the years –
Until it broke the waters, close
To my face, salt splash burning my eyes
Awake.

Birds gather from nowhere to greet it,
Screaming their glee, flapping cruel wings.
I too was a morsel of flesh when first drowned
At sea, Turner's smile shrunk like a worm's
Sudden contraction; strange words spat
From that gentle face that so often kissed us,
His favoured boys, in quiet corners,
Unseen passages, and when cold night winds
Growled outside, curled us warmly to his bed,
Like my mother, when fevers starch my blood
And I lie dazed, barely able to cry
For weakness, and she buries me in the blackness
Of her flesh, like the danja seeds my
Father is always planting in dark soil
Which sprout so quickly and grow as tall
As I awake now and walk, first stumbling,
Soon hopping with my friends to clearings
In the bush, special trees we climb to scout
For enemies, whom we will startle
With a torrent of twigs and fruit.

Birds I call by their plumage and cry
As these hundred years and more I have made
Names for places dwelt in, people forgotten:
Words are all I have left of my eyes,
Words of my own dreaming and those that Turner
Primed in my mouth. I float eyeless, indelibly,
My mind a garment of invention. Birds circle
At the bounty, vengeful, but I call them
Gentle names – Flambeau, Sulsi, Aramanda.
This one, arrogant in beauty, feathers
Blown loose, I baptise Tanje after the strumpet
Of our village. See how it reaches with bright wings
And beak, but a sudden wave beats it back, the child
Floats towards me, bloodied at first, but the sea
Will cleanse it. It has bleached me too of colour,
Painted me gaudy, dabs of ebony,
An arabesque of blues and vermilions,
Sea-quats cling to my body like gorgeous
Ornaments. I have become the sea's whore,
Yielding.

What sleep will leave me restless when I wake?
What mindfulness that nothing has remained
Original? There could have been some small
And monumental faith. Even the leper
Conserves each grain of skin, the aged
Grin to display a tooth sensuously
Preserved in gum, memorial to festivity
And speech that mocks the present and the time
To come.

It broke the waters and made the years
Stir, not in faint murmurs but a whirlpool
That sucks me under with lust for the smell
Of earth and root and freshly burst fruit,
My breasts a woman's which I surrender
To my child-mouth, feeding my own hurt
For the taste of sugared milk, mantee seeds
Crushed, my mother dipping them in sweet paste,
Letting me lick her fingers afterwards.
This creature kicks alive in my stomach
Such dreams of family, this thing which I cannot
Fathom, resembling a piece of ragged flesh,
Though human from the shape of its head,
Its half-formed eyes, seeming jaw and as yet
Sealed lips. Later it confirmed its breed,
Tugging my hair spitefully, startling me
With obscene memory. 'Nigger!' it cried, seeing
Through the sea's disguise as only children can,
Recognising me below my skin long since
Washed clean of the colour of sin, scab, smudge,
Pestilence, death, rats that carry plague,
Darkness such as blots the sky when locusts swarm.

The sea has brought me tribute from many lands,
Chests of silver, barrels of tobacco, sugar-loaves,
Swords with gleaming handles, crucifixes set in pearls
Which, marvelled at, but with the years grown rusty
And mouldy, abandoned – cheap and counterfeit
    goods:
The sea has mocked and beggared me for centuries,
Except for scrolls in different letterings
Which, before they dissolve, I decipher
As best I can. These, and the babbling
Of dying sailors, are my means to languages
And the wisdom of other tribes. Now the sea
Has delivered a child sought from the moon in years
Of courtship, when only the light from that silent
Full eye saw me whilst many ships passed by
Indifferently. She hides behind a veil
Like the brides of our village but watches me
In loneliness and grief for that vast space
That still carries my whisper to her ears,
Vaster than the circumference of the sea
That so swiftly drowned my early cries
In its unending roar. There is no land
In sight, no voice carries from that land,
My mother does not answer, I cannot hear her
Calling, as she did when I dragged myself
To the bank of the pond, my head a pool
And fountain of blood, and she runs to me
Screaming, plucks me up with huge hands,
Lays me down on land, as the sea promised
In early days, clasped and pitched me sideways
In the direction of our village, my dazed mind
Thought, across a distance big beyond even
Turner's grasp (he sketches endless numbers

In his book, face wrinkled in concentration
Like an old seal's mouth brooding in crevices
Of ice for fish; like my father
Counting beads at the end of each day,
Reckoning which calf was left abandoned
In the savannah, lost from the herd, eaten
By wild beasts. He checks that we are parcelled
In equal lots, men divided from women,
Chained in fours and children subtracted
From mothers. When all things tally
He snaps the book shut, his creased mouth
Unfolding in a smile, as when, entering
His cabin, mind heavy with care, breeding
And multiplying percentages, he beholds
A boy dishevelled on his bed). For months
It seemed to speed me to a spot where my mother
Waited, wringing her hands, until I woke to find
Only sea. Months became years and I forgot
The face of my mother, the plaid cloth
Tied around her neck, the scars on her forehead,
The silver nose-ring which I tugged, made her start,
Nearly rolling me from her lap but catching me
In time, and when I cried out in panic
Of falling, pinned me tightly, always,
To her bosom. Now I am loosed
Into the sea, I no longer call,
I have even forgotten the words.
Only the moon remains, watchful and loving
Across a vast space.

Sometimes half her face grows dark, she sulks
Impatient of my arms, all my entreaties
Grappled in a storm of rain; nothing will soothe her
Then, she cries herself to sleep or curves
Like a sickle that will wake the sky's throat,
Or curls her lip in scorn of me, a mere unborn
With insufficient cowrie shells, when others,
Men, substantial, beseech her favours
With necklaces of coloured glass to loop
Around her breasts, men of presence, neither ghost
Nor portent of a past or future life
Such as I am, now. Sometimes her cheeks are puffed,
Her face lopsided, and I think I must have
Blasted her in some lover's rage; my hand,
Two centuries and more lifeless, clenched in quick
Hate, reached endlessly to bruise her face.
She disappears behind clouds for many nights.
A sudden thought writhes: she might be dead,
I might never subject her again.

It was not her going but the manner of it,
Like Turner's hand gripping my neck,
Pushing me towards the edge, that no noise
Comes from my mouth, no lamentation
As I fall towards the sea, my breath held
In shock until the waters quell me.
Struggle came only after death, the flush
Of betrayal, and hate hardening my body
Like cork, buoying me when I should have sunk
And come to rest on the sea's bed among
The dregs of creatures without names
Which roamed these waters before human birth:
Jaws that gulped in shoals, demons of the universe
Now grin like clowns, tiny fish dart
Between the canyons of their teeth. I should have sunk
To these depths, where terror is transformed into
Comedy, where the sea, with an undertaker's
Touch, soothes and erases pain from the faces
Of drowned sailors, unpastes flesh from bone
With all its scars, boils, stubble, marks
Of debauchery.

I gather it in with dead arms, like harvest-time
We trooped into the fields at first light,
The lame, the hungry and frail, young men
Snorting like oxen, women trailing stiff
Cold children through mist that seeps from strange
Wounds in the land. We float like ghosts to fields
Of corn. All day I am a small boy
Nibbling at whatever grain falls from
My mother's breast as she bends and weaves
Before the crop, hugging a huge bundle
Of cobs to her body, which flames
In the sun, which blinds me as I look up
From her skirt, which makes me reach like a drowning
Man gropes at the white crest of waves, thinking it
Rope. I can no longer see her face
In the blackness. The sun has reaped my eyes.
I struggle to find her in the blackness
At the bottom of the sea where the brightest
Sunken treasure barely keeps its glow.

I gather it to my body, this grain,
This morsel slipped from the belly of moon,
And name it Turner and will instruct it
In the knowledge of landscapes learnt as the ship
Plunged towards another world we never reached.
The grown-ups cried in the darkness of the hold
But we lay freely in his bed, gazed at
Pictures on his wall. He held a lamp
Up to his country, which I never saw,
In spite of his promises, but in images
Of hedgerows that stalked the edge of fields,
Briars, vines, gouts of wild flowers: England's
Robe unfurled, prodigal of ornament,
Victorious in spectacle, like the oaks
That stride across the land, gnarled in battle
With storms, lightning, beasts that claw and burrow
In their trunks. A rabbit starts at footsteps,
Scoots away. I walk along a path shaded
By beech; curved branches form a canopy, protect
Me from the stare of men with fat hands
Feeling my weight, prying in my mouth,
Bidding. The earth is soft here, glazed with leaves,
The path ends at a brook stippled with waterflies,
But no reflection when I gaze into it,
The water will not see me, nor the villagers
In whose midst I stray, pausing before
The butcher's shop hung with goose and pheasant,
But its window will not see me though it shines
With other faces. This old one with silver
Hair leaking from a bonnet I follow home
Through a cobbled street. In her basket
A crusty loaf wrapped in fresh white cloth:
Herself. I know her, but she stares through me,

Opens the door, disappears. I linger
At many gates, wanting to be greeted.
The elders and the young, all day I follow them
Through village green, marketplace and church
Where, my eyes accustomed to the gloom, behold
Turner nailed to a tree, naked for all to see,
His back broken and splayed like the spine
Of his own book, blood leaking like leaves
From his arms and waist, but no one among
The silent worshippers hears me cry out
In pity and surprise.

Only Manu knew, stuffed with the yam
Of supplicants. He squats in the midst
Of their gifts of dozi, plantains, cola seeds,
Rubs his belly and yawns. He will summon up
The spirits in his own time. He chews
A twig, picks the stodge from his teeth, spits,
Whilst his women, fat with child or afterbirth
Mix the ancient ingredients, arrange
The sacred bowls around his body.
He looks on hazily, burps. The villagers
Wriggle their ears but the spirits stay silent
Until he darts his hands out at a bowl,
Scoops up red jelly, daubs it on his face,
Howls. The villagers scatter. They gather
In the gloom at the back of his hut, whilst
The sun pours through a window upon his head
Like a libation. Between shrieks he prophesies
The stranger who will bring rain to fertilise
The crops, and lamentation in the land,
Who will bless us and decapitate the gods,
Who will make marks on the earth with his finger,
Writing boundaries, who will fashion metal
With new sorcery to kill us in herds,
Who will deliver us from evil and disease,
Teach us new ways to reap and speak.
Was it a boy's dream that Manu foretold
Native schemes against this stranger?
Premeditations to spear his side, spill
The magic from his wrists, sacrifice
Him to a withered babla tree that will
Soak the blood and flourish once more
With the knowledge of our ancient tribe?
Like Turner's book, blistered in its covers

But paged with freshly-inked figures, a thicket
Of strokes, and dots like pits that trap even
The fleetest of our hunters, twists his foot,
Makes him die on his own spear?

'Nigger,' it cries, naming me from some hoard
Of superior knowledge, its tongue a viper's nest
Guarding a lore buried by priests, philosophers,
Fugitives, which I will still ransack
For pearls and coral beads to drape around
Its body, covering the sores that the sea
Bubbles on its skin, its strangulated neck
Issuing like an eel from its chest. 'Nigger,'
It cries, sensing its own deformity.
I look into its eyes to see my own coves,
My skin pitted and gathered like waves of sand.
I have become the sea's craft and will so shape
This creature's bone and cell and word beyond
Memory of obscene human form, but instead
It made me heed its distress at being
Human and alive, its anger at my
Coaxing it awake. For ever, it seemed,
Curled at my breast it drifted between death
And another mood, the waves slapping its face
Like my mother's hands summoning me back
To myself, at the edge of the pond. I stare
Into its face as into a daedal
Seed which Manu would hold up to the sky
For portents of flood, famine, or the crop
Of new births to supplement our tribe,
But even Manu could not prophesy
The shapes of death revolving in its eyes:
Bullwhips that play upon the backs of slaves
Hauling pillars of stone to a spot divined
By sorcerers whose throw of dice from whimsical
Hands appoints thousands to their deaths, arranges
Human bones like hieroglyphs to tell a prurient
Future age the ancient formulae of Empire.

A solitary vulture dips into one's fresh breast
As into an ink-well, wipes its beak upon
Another's parchment skin, writing its own
Version of events, whilst Pharaoh sleeps in cloths
Scented in the flow of female sacrifice.
Until a slave arose from the dead,
Cracking the seal of his mouth, waking
The buried with forbidden words. 'Revolt,'
He thundered, 'emancipation, blood', darkening
The sky with his lust, irrigating
Their stomachs, blooming courage in their skulls.
An army of sticks and sharpened flints flocked
Across the sands like ragged cacti, ripping
Down tents, encampments, cities, massacring
The men, scavenging the bellies of their wives
For scraps of joy. Wherever they settled
They made new deserts and new slaves. 'Revolt,'
He whispered, lifting aloft the Pharaoh's
Crown from a head chopped clean at the neck,
    hollowed
Into a drinking gourd. They cheered even as
They sipped at each other's throats in nostalgia
For death, except a child who slipped and limped
Away from the lap of men who loved him
Too much, broke him each night in frustration
Of their lives. Children appeared everywhere,
Strewn like dung at the root of palms
As if to fertilise and succour them
Against the desert, to memorialise
In the spur of leaves the veins
Once flowing with maternity. Everywhere,
Children trailing behind caravans heading
North to the auction tents of Arabia,
Sucking the air for any nipple of moisture.

Shall I call to it in the forgotten
Voice of my mother, this thing drawn yet
Struggling to break free, seeking a mirage
Of breast yet sniffing me for traces of what
I am, slave like itself, nigger made impotent,
Hurt by different hands in different ages?
Shall I call to it in the distant voice
Of my mother, even as sound lingers
In a conch from which flesh and substance has been
Scooped? She bids her famished children eat
Of their father's labour, at tables laden
With meats, spices of odalan, nutmeg,
Cinnamon, and berries that multiply on vines,
Yams, jilips, achroes, blue aramantines
Picked lavishly from the soil which my father
Works in communion with other men.
Shall I summon up such a pageant of fruit,
Peopling a country with musicians, dancers,
Poets, and our simple deities of stone
And wattle, which Turner vandalised
With a great sweep of his sword in search
Of his own fables, teaching us instead
The value of the grit that gleamed commonly
At the bottom of streams which boys would spurn
In quest of pebbles more rounded and weighty
For their slings?

Shall I call to it even as the dead
Survive catastrophe to speak in one
Redemptive and prophetic voice, even
As a jackal breathing into bone
Rouses familiar song? Shall I suckle
It on tales of resurrected folk,
Invent a sister, and another, as Manu would,
Pursing his lips so all the wrinkles
On his face gathered like spokes around the hub
Of his mouth and he would stare backwards
Through his eye sockets into himself whilst
We waited at his feet in dread of the word
That would spin suddenly from his throat,
Cartwheel towards us, making us want
To scatter, but we remained rooted
At his feet in stunned obedience
To his booming voice and his quivering
Fat manitou's body pouring forth sweat
Enough to water all the animals
Herded in the savannah? The first word
Shot from his mouth, he stretched out his lizard's
Tongue after it, retrieved it instantly
On the curled tip, closed his mouth, chewed.
     When he
Grinded the word into bits he began his tale,
One grain at a time fed to our lips
Endlessly, the sack of his mouth bulging
With wheat, until we grew sluggish and tame
With overeating, and fell asleep, his life-
Long tale to be continued in dreams.
Each morning, the milking of the cow done,
Our father deposited us in Manu's hut
For instruction. He resumed from the previous

Day, his hands still agile as he declaimed,
His eyes frantically bright as if he was cursed
To stay awake until his story ended. Only
Then would the gods send him sleep, so peaceful
And dark a sleep: the serpent's whisper, the lover's
Melody, the prisoner wailing the hours
To his execution, the startled laughter
Of the reprieved, no such sounds of triumph or loss
Which he mimicked in his tale would awaken him.
Now restlessly he sleeps, his duty unfulfilled,
His hands still gripped to the ghost of the sword
Turner insinuated into his belly,
Withdrew, sheathed, his mouth still open as if
Wanting to continue his tale. Only flies
Perform his obsequies, gathering on his tongue
To hum eulogies to our magician,
Our childhood, our promise, our broken
Word.

Two sisters I will make in Manu's memory,
Lead both to riches and to barrenness,
One and the same pathway Manu prophesied,
His voice lowered to a mysterious whisper
As he told that time future was neither time past
Nor time present, but a rupture so complete
That pain and happiness will become one, death
And freedom, barrenness and riches. He
Ripped away his jouti necklace without warning,
The beads rolled from the thread, scattered like
    coloured
Marbles and we scrambled to gather them,
Each child clutching an accidental handful
Where before they hung in a sequence of hues
Around his neck, the pattern of which only he
Knew – from his father and those before – to
    preserve.
The jouti lay in different hands, in different
Colours. We stared bleakly at them and looked
To Manu for guidance, but he gave no instruction
Except – and his voice gathered rage and
    unhappiness –
That in the future time each must learn to live
Beadless in a foreign land; or perish.
Or each must learn to make new jouti,
Arrange them by instinct, imagination, study
And arbitrary choice into a pattern
Pleasing to the self and to others
Of the scattered tribe; or perish. Each
Will be barren of ancestral memory
But each endowed richly with such emptiness
From which to dream, surmise, invent, immortalise.

Though each will wear different coloured beads
Each will be Manu, the source and future
Chronicles of our tribe.

The first of my sisters, stout, extravagant,
I will name Rima. Even as a child
She tempts fate, tempts the hand of my father
Blossoming at her face, but she will still deny
The sin and multiply his faith in her;
The more she doubts, the more convinced he grows
Of her purity. Afterwards she bites into
His reparation of jhal cakes with
Playful teeth. She will steal my spears, my warriors,
My fortifications. She will interrupt the most
Careful of ambushes with a stomp of her feet,
Mashing down escarpments, gouging deep holes
In the battleground with her unhewn toenail.
I report her to my mother who slaps
Me instead for playing at killing,
Nor will my father heed but turns his face
To the earth and hoes like a beaten man.
He has been vanquished by her freedom.
She is wayward and sucks her teeth,
Talks above the voices of the elders,
Will not shield her eyes before them.
When she grows up she will love women
More fiercely than men and die at childbirth
With her husband fanning her and marvelling
At the deed, the village idiot whom she
Married out of jest and spite. She is all
The valour and anguish of our tribe,
My beloved, and we bury her
In a space kept only for those who have
Uttered peculiarly, those who have
Guarded our faith by prophecy, who have
Called out in the voices of the hunter
Or betrayer so we could recognise

Him beforehand. And the women will come
Bearing stones, each one placed on her grave
A wish for her protection against kidnapping,
Rape, pregnancy, beatings, men, all men:
Turner.

The first of my sisters I have named Rima.
I endow her with a clear voice, fingers
That coax melody from the crudest instrument,
Melody that brings tears from men, even Turner
Who sits cross-legged before her, beguiled by song.
Afterwards he will go to Ellar, the second-born,
Whom he will ravish with whips, stuff rags
In her mouth to stifle the rage, rub salt
Into the stripes of her wounds in slow ecstatic
Ritual trance, each grain caressed and secreted
Into her ripped skin like a trader placing each
Counted coin back into his purse. Her flesh is open
Like the folds of a purse, she receives
His munificence of salt. By the time he has done
With her he has taken the rage from her mouth.
It opens and closes. No word comes. It opens
And closes. It keeps his treasures.
It will never tell their secret burial places.
He is content. He has made her the keeper
Of his treasures. He unties her hands and lets
Her go. Each night he sits in rapture before Rima,
Weeping.

Turner crammed our boys' mouths too with riches,
His tongue spurting strange potions upon ours
Which left us dazed, which made us forget
The very sound of our speech. Each night
Aboard ship he gave selflessly the nipple
Of his tongue until we learnt to say profitably
In his own language, *we desire you, we love
You, we forgive you.* He whispered eloquently
Into our ears even as we wriggled beneath him,
Breathless with pain, wanting to remove his hook
Implanted in our flesh. The more we struggled
Ungratefully, the more steadfast his resolve
To teach us words. He fished us patiently,
Obsessively, until our stubbornness gave way
To an exhaustion more complete than Manu's
Sleep after the sword bore into him
And we repeated in a trance the words
That shuddered from him: *blessed, angelic,
Sublime*; words that seemed to flow endlessly
From him, filling our mouths and bellies
Endlessly.

'Nigger,' it cries, loosening from the hook
Of my desire, drifting away from
My body of lies. I wanted to teach it
A redemptive song, fashion new descriptions
Of things, new colours fountaining out of form.
I wanted to begin anew in the sea
But the child would not bear the future
Nor its inventions, and my face was rooted
In the ground of memory, a ground stampeded
By herds of foreign men who swallow all its fruit
And leave a trail of dung for flies
To colonise; a tongueless earth, bereft
Of song except for the idiot witter
Of wind through a dead wood. 'Nigger'
It cries, naming itself, naming the gods,
The earth and its globe of stars. It dips
Below the surface, frantically it tries to die,
To leave me beadless, nothing and a slave
To nothingness, to the white enfolding
Wings of Turner brooding over my body,
Stopping my mouth, drowning me in the yolk
Of myself. There is no mother, family,
Savannah fattening with cows, community
Of faithful men; no elders to foretell
The conspiracy of stars; magicians to douse
Our burning temples; no moon, no seed,
No priests to appease the malice of the gods
By gifts of precious speech – rhetoric antique
And lofty, beyond the grasp and cunning
Of the heathen and conquistador –
Chants, shrieks, invocations uttered on the first
Day spontaneously, from the most obscure
Part of the self when the first of our tribe

Awoke, and was lonely, and hazarded
Foliage of thorns, earth that still smouldered,
The piercing freshness of air in his lungs
In search of another image of himself.
No savannah, moon, gods, magicians
To heal or curse, harvests, ceremonies,
No men to plough, corn to fatten their herds,
No stars, no land, no words, no community,
No mother.

THE OLD MAP

Empty treasure chests dumped from departed ships
And jettisoned slaves washed
Into an arc from Jamaica to Guiana.
Islands aborted from the belly of sea
Forever unborn in rock and swamp.
Other fragments rot in the sun
Like cane chewed and spat
From coolie mouth.
Haiti is a crab with broken claw.
Cuba droops in fear at the foot of America.
Blue is deep and everywhere of European eye,
Green of seamen's hopes and gangrene,
Yellow of the palm of dead Amerindian
Unyielding gold.

EL DORADO

Juncha slowly dying of jaundice
Or yellow fever or blight or jumbie or neighbour's
    spite,
No one knows why he turns the colour of cane.

Small boys come to peep, wondering
At the hush of the death-hut
Until their mothers bawl them out.

Skin flaking like goldleaf
Casts a halo round his bed.
He goes out in a puff of gold dust.

Bathed like a newborn child by the women.
Laid out in his hammock in the yard.
Put out to feel the last sun.

They bury him like treasure,
The coolie who worked two shillings all day
But kept his value from the overseer.

SONG OF THE CREOLE GANG WOMEN

1st Woman

Wuk, nuttin bu wuk
Maan noon an night nuttin bu wuk
Booker own me patacake
Booker own me pickni.
Pain, nuttin bu pain
Waan million tous'ne acre cane.
O since me baan – juk! juk! juk! juk! juk!
So sun in me eye like taan
So Booker saach deep in me flesh
Kase Booker own me rass
An Booker own me cutlass –
Bu me dun cuss . . . Gaad leh me na cuss no mo!

Caan in me finga, caan in me foot-battam . . .

Chorus

Dosay an mittae, dosay an mittae,
Booker put e mout on me like pirae.

2nd Woman

Kiss-kiss-kidee! Kiss-kiss-kiss-kideee!
So wind a howl from de haat o bush
Like bird mesh, tear up on twig.
Hear, hear how e'ya cry, cry, how e'ya bleed on de air,
An bruk up over bud aweh hooman, sickle in haan,
Sweep an sway all day to e saang
Babee strap like burden to we back.
Kiss-kiss-kidee! Kiss-kiss-kiss-kideee!

Chorus

Dutty-skin, distress, shake aff we babee
When we reach wataside shake aff we patakee.

3rd Woman

Is true everyting stall, gape, bleed,
Like crappau foot squash jess as e'ya leap?

4th Woman

Everyting tie up, haat, lung, liva, an who go loose me caad? –
Shaap, straight, sudden like pimpla, cut free
An belly buss out like blood-flow a shriek?
Or who saaf haan, saaf-flesh finga?
Or who go paste e mout on me wound, lick, heal, like
    starapple suck?

5th Woman

Look a de sun how e fix in de sky like taskmasta eye,
A de coconut-tree dat watch over we like overseer
Treaten fo spill e load on we maiden head . . .
Me tust, dust an vinega choke me mout, sweat leak over
    me like gutta-wata
Heat a hatch louse in me hair . . .

Chorus

Leh we go sit dung riverside, dip, dodo, die –
Shade deep in cool deh.

(They move off, repeating these lines with mournful
voices, that gradually fade out. A deep silence.)

Work, nothing but work/ Morning noon and night nothing but work/ Booker owns my cunt/ Booker owns my children/ Pain, nothing but pain/ One million thousand acres cane/ O since I was born – stab! stab! stab! stab! stab!/ So sun in my eye like thorn/ So Booker searches deep in my flesh/ Because Booker owns my arse/ And Booker owns my cutlass/ But I'm done with cursing, God let me not curse any more/ Corn in my finger, corn in my foot-bottom.

Dosay and mittae, dosay and mittae/ Booker puts his mouth on me like piranha.

Kiss-kiss-kidee! Kiss-kiss-kiss-kideee!/ So wind howls from the heart of bush/ Like a bird meshed, torn upon twigs/ Hear how it cries, cries, how it bleeds on the air/ And broken over buds we women, sickles in hand/ Sweep and sway all day to its song/ Babies strapped like burdens to our backs/ Kiss-kiss-kidee! Kiss-kiss-kiss-kideee!

Dirty-skin, distressed, shake off our babies/ When we reach waterside shake off our cunts.

Is it true everything stalls, gapes, bleeds/ Like frog foot squashes just as it is about to leap?

Everything tied up, heart, lung, liver, and who will loose my cords?/ Sharp, straight, sudden, like pimpla, cut them free/ And belly bursts out like blood-flow shrieking?/ Or whose soft hand, soft-fleshed finger?/ Or who will paste his mouth on my wound, lick, heal, like starapple suck?

Look at the sun how it's fixed in the sky like a taskmaster's eye/ At the coconut-tree that watches over us like an overseer/ Threatening to spill his load on our maiden heads . . ./ I'm thirsty, dust and vinegar choke my mouth, sweat leaks over me like gutter-water/ Heat hatches lice in my hair.

Let's go sit down riverside, dip, sleep, die/ Shade deep in cool there.

---

* *Booker:* British sugar company that owned Guyana

SLAVE SONG

Tie me haan up.
Juk out me eye.
Haal me teet out
So me na go bite.
Put chain rung me neck.
Lash me foot tight.
Set yu daag fo gyaad
Maan till nite –

Bu yu caan stap me cack floodin in de goldmine
Caan stap me cack splashin in de sunshine!

Whip me till me bleed
Till me beg.
Tell me how me hanimal
African orang-utan
Tell me how me cannibal
Fit fo slata fit fo hang.
Slice waan lip out
Waan ear an waan leg –

Bu yu caan stap me cack dippin in de honeypot
Drippin at de tip an happy as a Hottentot!

Look how e'ya leap from bush to bush like a black crappau
Seeking out a watahole,
Blind by de sunflare, tongue like a dussbowl –
See how e'ya sip laang an full an slow!

Till e swell an heavy, stubban, chupit, full o sleep
Like camoudie swalla calf an stretch out in de grass, content,
Full o peace . . .
Hibiscus bloom, a cool breeze blow
An from a hill a wataflow
Canary singin saaf an low . . .

Is so when yu dun dream she pink tit,
Totempole she puss,
Leff yu teetmark like a tattoo in she troat!

She gi me taat
She gi me wife
So tear out me liver
Or stake me haat
Me still gat life!

———————————

Tie my hands up/ Pierce my eyes/ Haul my teeth out/ So I'll not bite./ Put chains around my neck/ Lash my feet tight/ Set your dogs to guard/ Morning till night –

But you can't stop my cock flooding in the goldmine/ Can't stop my cock splashing in the sunshine!

Whip me till I bleed/ Till I beg./ Tell me I'm an animal/ An African orangutan/ Tell me I'm a cannibal/ Fit only to slaughter or to hang/ Slice one lip out/ One ear and one leg –

But you can't stop my cock dipping in the honeypot,/ Dripping at the tip and happy as a Hottentot!

Look how he leaps from bush to bush like a black toad/ Seeking out a waterhole/ Blind by the sunflare, tongue like a dust-bowl –/ See how he sips long and full and slow!

Till he's swollen and heavy, stubborn, dazed, full of sleep/ Like camoudie snake after swallowing a calf, stretched out in the grass, content/ Full of peace . . . / Hibiscus bloom, a cool breeze blows/ And from a hill a waterflow/ Canaries singing soft and low . . .

It's so when you've done dreamt her pink nipples/ Totempoled her cunt/ Left your teeth mark like a tattoo in her throat!

She gives me thought/ She gives me wife/ So tear out my liver/ Or stake my heart/ I'll still have life.

47

NIGHTMARE

Bruk dung de door!
Waan gang sweat-stink nigga
Drag she aff she bed
Wuk pun she
Crack she head
Gi she jigga
Tween she leg!

Dem chase she backdam:
Waan gang cane-stiff cack
Buss she tail till she blue an black
Till she crawl tru de mud an she bawl an she beg.

Dem haul she canal-bank like bush-haag
Cut she troat over de dark surging wata
When dem dun suck dem raise dem red mout to de moon
An mek saang,

Deep in de night when crappau call an cush-cush
Crawl dung hole, lay dem egg in de earth
When camoudie curl rung calf dat just drap
An black bat flap-flap-flap tru de bush . . .

Wet she awake, cuss de daybreak!

Batter down the door!/ One gang of sweaty, stinking niggers/ Drag her off her bed/ Work upon her/ Crack her head/ Give her jigga/ Between her legs.

They chase her backdam/ One gang of cane-stiff cocks/ Lash her buttocks till they're black and blue/ Till she crawls through the mud and she bawls and she begs.

They haul her to the canal-bank like a bush-hog/ Cut her throat over the dark surging waters/ When they finish sucking they raise their red mouths to the moon/ And make song,

Deep in the night when crappau call and cush-cush/ Crawl down holes, lay their eggs in the earth/ When camoudie snake curls round calf that's just dropped/ And black bats flap-flap-flap through the bush

Wet she awakes, cursing the daybreak!

REBEL LOVE

When first he put his black hand to her breast, waiting
The whiplash, white men bellowing pain,
Pigs with bruised testicles battering their pen,
He dreamt a cornucopia of slaves poured overboard,
The suck of sharks, bleached, boned,
Washed up in Berbice,
He dreamt the dance of flames on coolieman skin
Running amok, screamed, smouldered to ash
To fertilise the canefields of Demerara,
He dreamt the dogs unloosed howling through the bush
Where, drunk with disobedience, stumbling,
Abandoned to her flesh,
He fell and lay
Still.

MIRANDA

His black bony peasant body
Stalk of blighted cane
In dry earth.

I will blot out the tyrant sun
Cleanse you in the raincloud of my body
In the secrecy of night set you supple and erect.

And wiped him with the moist cloth of her tongue
Like a new mother licking clean its calf
And hugged milk from her breast to his cracked mouth.

That when he woke he cried to dream again
Of the scent of her maternity
The dream of the moon of her deep spacious eye

Sea-blue and bountiful
Beyond supplication or conquest
A frail slave vessel wracked upon a mere pebble of her
    promise.

And the sun resumed its cruelty
And the sun shook with imperial glee
At the fantasy.

LOVE SONG

Moon-eye
Blue like blue-saki wing,
Moon-eye, all maan in me mine . . .

Black man cover wid estate ash
E ead haad an dry like calabash,
Dut in e nose-hole, in e ear-hole,
Dut in e soul, in e battie-hole.

All
day
sun
bun
tongue
bun
all
day
troat
cut
haat
hut
wuk na dun, na dun, na dun!
Hack! Hack! Hack! Hack!
Cutlass slip an cut me cack!

Tank Gaad six a'clack!
Me go home
An me go bade
An me go comb
An me go rock
In hammock
Cassava, pepperpot,
Drink some rum an coconut!

An when me soul saaf an me eye wet
An de breeze blow an me eye shet
An de bakle na ga mo rum
Den leh yuh come
An tek me wey, wheh
Chain na deh, wheh
Cane na deh.
Leh yuh come wid milk in yuh breast an yuh white troat bare
Wid bangle on yuh haan an bell rung yuh waiss
Leh yuh come wid oil an perfume an lace . . .

Moon-eye
Blue like blue-saki wing,
Silk frack tumble an splash on me face like wata-fall
An yuh dance an yuh call
In de night.

Moon-eye/ Blue like blue-saki wing/ Moon-eye, all morning in my mind.

Black man covered with estate-ash/ His head hard and dry like calabash/ Dirt in his nostrils, in his ears/ Dirt in his soul, in his arse-hole.

All/ day/ sun/ burns/ tongue/ burns/ all/ day/ throat/ cut/ heart/ hurt/ work's never done, never done, never done./ Hack! Hack! Hack! Hack!/ Cutlass slips and cuts your cock.

Thank God for six o'clock/ I go home/ And I'll bathe/ And I'll comb/ And I'll rock/ In hammock/ Cassava, pepperpot/ Drink some rum and coconut!

And when my soul's soft and my eyes wet/ And the breeze blows and my eyes shut/ And the bottle has no more rum/ Then come/ And take me away, where/ there's no chain/ there's no cane/ Come with milk in your breast and your white throat bare/ With bangles on your hands and bells round your waist/ Come with oil and perfume and lace.

Moon-eye/ Blue like blue-saki wing/ Silk frock tumbles and splashes on my face like waterfall/And you dance and you call/ In the night.

THE SEXUAL WORD

She dreaded the naivety
Of longing for rebirth,
Beheld him stuttering out his dream
Of journeys ended:
The howling oceanic thrust of history
That heaved forth savages in strange canoes
Weighed with magical cannon and muzzle and ankle-chain,
Stilled
To a pool in his eye
Through which he saw
The solitary quay
The new seed.

He burnt his mind in acid of his own alchemy
Urging song from his hurt mouth
Desperate to colonise her
In images of gold and fertility
To remake her from his famished rib
To redeem her from the white world
That would reduce him to mute captivity.

She refused the embrace of fantasy,
Unable to be torn up, transplanted,
Stripped, raped, broken and made to bear
Beautiful bastard fruit –
She could not endure the repetition
Necessary for new beginning

Yet was ravished by the poetry.

IMPOTENCE

He waits below you
Like a deep earth hole
That snakes and eyeless insects make
Through shame of revelation.
The blue moon-motherness of your eye
Watches over broken adolescence
Suffocating in its tight black skin.

Swollen with gold
The imperial cane
Stampedes the land
Sun-god and overseer
To whom he pays
Tribute of his mother.

Now, in the blueness of your gaze
He dreams
The interminable sea,
Strapped horizontal to the deck,
The interminable sky,
Now, in the glow and gentle touch of your hair
He dreams
The stiff pike of cane
The failed insurrection.

MA TALKING WORDS

You only fool yourself when you say
The woman shallow as the water
She cleanse she make-up in
And you out of your precious depth.
Fact is the world want she
And all you can do is curse cut throat and despair
Or more crazy still
Write poetry:
That is dream and air!
You can't make pickni from word
Howsoever beautiful or raging:
The world don't know word.

Next time you lay down with she
And the white flesh wrench and bite like ratmouth
And she moaning fill you with pride,
But after you feel suck dry, throw-away like eggshell or
    seed,
Think that all-body here know your heart still flesh with
    good
And this village ground never grow more bright boy
    before
Who move out from mud and walk England
And we who stay back
Mash-mouth and crack
Still feed in you.

And how she go understand all that burden and fruit
You bear for we?
And how she go crave your soul and seed
Who always eat plenty
From different pot?

Book learning you got,
But history done dead, hard like teeth and bone
And white people don't want heal their own scar or hear
    their own story
And you can't hug them with bruk hand
Or lash sense in them with overseer stick.

Young and fresh and pretty
She swallow the world and get belly,
Rub lipstick on she mouth and make joke,
Nightlong music shake she foot.
All man a-take from she and go their way
Whilst stupid you want stay
Pan love like diamond from dirt
And dream that the world know word.

ON HER UNFAITHFULNESS

They were not accustomed to space
Except a piece of porthole showing sky
Imagined, or shovelled into logies
Doorways cracked open to cane-fields choked with work.
His mother dropped a new child every year
And all affection was crowded out.
His mother was a sackful of crabs in her womb, scratching
Up, mashing
Up, clawing
For air.
Now you must surely see
Why he seeks
The wide space and sole portion of your heart
In which to be singularly free.

And all my furious talk of fidelity
Was because of that you see.

---

* *logies:* Old slave barracks which housed newly arrived indentured
Indian labourers

CATCHING CRABS

Ruby and me stalking savannah
Crab season with cutlass and sack like big folk.
Hiding behind stones or clumps of bush
Crabs locked knee-deep in mud mating
And Ruby seven years old feeling strange at the sex
And me horrified to pick them up
Plunge them into the darkness of bag,
So all day we scout to catch the lonesome ones
Who don't mind cooking because they got no prospect
Of family, and squelching through the mud,
Cutlass clearing bush at our feet,
We come home tired slow, weighed down with plenty
Which Ma throw live into boiling pot piece-piece.
Tonight we'll have one big happy curry feed,
We'll test out who teeth and jaw strongest
Who will grow up to be the biggest
Or who will make most terrible cannibal.

We leave behind a mess of bones and shell
And come to England and America
Where Ruby hustles in a New York tenement
And me writing poetry at Cambridge,
Death long catch Ma, the house boarded up
Breeding wasps, woodlice in its dark-sack belly:
I am afraid to walk through weed yard,
Reach the door, prise open, look,
In case the pot still bubbles magical
On the fireside, and I see Ma
Working a ladle, slow –
Limbed, crustacean-old, alone,
In case the woodsmoke and curry steam
Burn my child-eye and make it cry.

FOR MA

Roll roti! roll roti! roll roti! roll roti!
Curry cookin in de karahee
Bora boilin wid de bagee
Woodsmoke sweet in me nose like agarbattee –
Ayuh wake up wake up ayuh pickni wake up ayuh man
Wid de sunshine in yu eye an de river a flow
An brung doves burstin from de trees an de kiskidees
An de whole savannah swimmin green an a glow!

Wata foh fetch battam-house foh daub fresh bucket foh
    mend clothes foh beat
Wake up ayuh pickni wuk na dun wuk foh duh
Cutlass foh shaap wood foh chap fence foh build dat bull
    bruk dung
Is wha da maan a stretch e haan an yaan foh!
Hear a cow baal in de yaad how dem swell wid milk-fraff
Goat a groan dem want go graze an sheep a caff-caff –
Ayuh wake up wake up time na deh foh cry time na deh
    foh laff
Hen a lay an cow a drap time na deh foh stap!

Roll roti! roll roti! roll roti! roll roti!/ Curry cooking in the karahie/ Bora boiling with the bagee/ Woodsmoke sweet in my nose like incense/ Wake up, wake up the lot of you, wake up you children, wake up you man/ With the sunshine in your eyes and the river flowing/ And brown doves bursting from the trees, and the kiskadees/ And the whole savannah swimming green and glowing!

Water to fetch, bottom-house to daub afresh, bucket to mend, clothes to beat/ Wake up you children, work's not done, work's to do/ Cutlass to sharpen, wood to chop, fence to rebuild that the bull broke down,/ What's that man stretching his hand and yawning for!/ Hear how the cows bawl in the yard, they're swollen with milk/ The goats groan, they want to graze, and sheep keep coughing./ Wake up you lot, wake up, there's no time to cry, there's no time to laugh/ Hens are laying, cows are bearing, there's no time to stop!

COOLIE MOTHER

Jasmattie live in bruk –
Down hut big like Bata shoe-box,
Beat clothes, weed yard, chop wood, feed fowl
For this body and that body and every blasted body,
Fetch water, all day fetch water like if the whole –
Whole slow-flowing Canje river God create
Just for *she* one own bucket.

Till she foot-bottom crack and she hand cut-up
And curse swarm from she mouth like red-ants
And she cough blood on the ground but mash it in:
Because Jasmattie heart hard, she mind set hard

To hustle save she one-one slow penny,
Because one-one dutty make dam cross the Canje
And she son Harilall *got* to go school in Georgetown,
Must wear clean starch pants, or they go laugh at he,
Strap leather on he foot, and he *must* read book,
Learn talk proper, take exam, go to England university,
Not turn out like he rum-sucker chamar dadee.

* *dutty:* piece of earth
* *chamar:* low-caste

COOLIE SON

(The Toilet Attendant Writes Home)

Taana boy, how you do?
How Shanti stay? And Sukhoo?
Mosquito still a-bite all-you?
Juncha dead true-true?
Mala bruk-foot set?
Food deh foh eat yet?

Englan nice, snow and dem ting,
A land dey say fit for a king,
Iceapple plenty on de tree and bird a-sing –
Is de beginning of what dey call 'The Spring'.

And I eating enough for all a-we
And reading book bad-bad.

But is what make Matam wife fall sick
And Sonnel cow suck dry wid tick?

Soon, I go turn lawya or dacta,
But, just now, passage money run out
So I tek lil wuk –
I is a Deputy Sanitary Inspecta,
Big-big office, boy! Tie round me neck!
Brand new uniform, one big bunch keys!
If Ma can see me now how she go please . . .

* *tek lil wuk:* taken some casual work

63

So me saary.
Bu when yu grow old an yu voice weak an yu mout
    dribble
An yu foot-battam crack,
Is too late
Foh seh saary.

Bu me still saary.

Kase me drink rum an beat yu
Young saaf wet-eye face.
Kase me gi yu big belly year after year
Nine pickni foh feed, an me run way wid sweet-hooman
Sport all me inheritance whore-house.
Kase yu wuk in de field maaning till night, bruise –
Up yu small haan an yu skin peel in de sun.
Kase when yu sit dung an roll roti, or rock baby in
    hammock,
Yu na sing glad-glad like odda hooman
How yu mout sour like aachar.

Me come back now, bu now yu old
An yu na know me
How yu mind weak
An yu eye dull.
Bu blood stir in me bady still when me look pun yu,
Like laang-time, when yu was me midnight bride,
Bright, fresh, hopeful, an me lay yu dung dunlopilla bed –
Downstairs dem a beat drum, dem a sing love saang, dem
    a dance in de firelight! . . .

An me saary bad!

So I'm sorry./ But when you've grown old, and your voice weak, and your mouth dribbling/ And the soles of your feet cracked/ It's too late/ To say sorry.

But I'm still sorry.

Because I drank rum and beat your/ Young, soft, wet-eyed face./ Because I made you pregnant year after year/ Nine mouths to feed, and I run off with sweet woman/ Sport all my inheritance in whore-house./ Because you had to work in the fields, from morning till night/ Bruising up your small hand, and the sun peeling your skin./ Because when you sat down to roll pancakes, or to rock baby in hammock/You didn't sing with gladness like other women/ How your mouth was sour like tamarind.

I've come back now, but now you're old/ And you don't know me/ How your mind's weak/ And your eyes dull/ But blood stirs in my body still when I look upon you/ Like long time ago, when you were my midnight bride/ Bright, fresh, hopeful, and I lay you upon the Dunlopillo bed –/ Downstairs they were beating drums, they were singing love songs, they were dancing in the firelight! . . .

And I'm truly sorry!

ELEGY

So yu lean over landing, early cole maaning
Old man, yu sick? Is wha do yu? Wha wraang?
An yu haan weak, tremble, an yu mout move
Bu word na deh, an yu eye stare out at de field, laang,
    laang,
Bu yu na see calf stir an struggle foh suck
An yu na hear high from jamoon tree bluesaki saang –
Is old yu old . . . is dah wha mek . . .

Snakeneck, Fisheye, Badman, Rich'ed,
Young yesterday, all a dem baais, Tiefman, Blackbattie,
    Goose,
Late late in de night ayuh drink rum ayuh beat drum,
Roast crab, curass, tell jumbie story till maaning come . . .
Is wheh dem deh? All lay up dem net, all put dung dem
    cutlass, all let dem sheep loose,
All dead!
An Jasmattie beating claat on de riverbank – tump! tump!
    tump! tump!
How she haan straang an she back straight an she bubby
    sweet sapadilla-brung!
Yu memba when yu fuss see she how yu troat lump?
How she young bady leap, leak blood, when yu roll she
    pun de grung? . . .

All dem slingshat buss, all dem fence bruk –
Dung, so jackass graze in dem vegetable gyaaden, bird a
    peck,
Fireside crack, an battamhouse, an puckni na blow, bellnay
    na wuk –
An is wha mek . . .?

So you lean over the banister, early cold morning/ Old man. Are you sick? What's the matter with you? What's wrong?/ And your hands are weak, trembling, and your mouth moves/ But there're no words, and your eye stares out at the field, long, long/ But you do not see the calves stir and struggle to suck/ And you do not hear the blue-saki's song high in the jamoon tree –/ It's old you're old, that's what it is.

Snakeneck, Fisheye, Badman, Richard/ Young yesterday all those boys, Thiefman, Blackarse, Goose/ Late late in the night you drank rum, you beat drums/ Roast crabs, curass, telling ghost stories till morning comes . . . /And where are they? All laid up their nets, put down their cutlasses, all let their sheep loose/ All dead!/ And Jasmattie beating clothes on the river-bank – thump! thump! thump! thump!/ How her hands are strong, and her back straight and her breasts sweet sapidilla – brown!/ You re-member how your throat lumped when you first saw her/ And how her young body leapt, leaked blood, when you rolled her on the ground? . . .

All their slingshots burst, all their fences broken/ Down, so animals graze unmolested in their vegetable gardens, and birds peck/ The fireside is cracked, and the bottomhouse, and no mouth blows the bellows, no hand works the rolling-pin/ And what makes things so?

SLAVEWOMAN'S SONG

Ya howl –
Hear how ya howl –
Tell me wha ya howl foh
Tell me noh?
Pickni?
Dem tek pickni way?
Wha dem do wid pickni
Mek yu knaack yu head wid stone
Bite yu haan like daag-bone?

Is husban mek yu halla gal?
Wha dem do wid maan
Mek yu daub yu face wid cow dung
Juk yu eye an chap yu tongue?
Dem trow am Demerara, feed am
    alligata?

Muma? Pupa? Africa?
Belly big wid Massa?

Ya howl –
Hear how ya howl –
Tell me wha ya howl foh
Tell me noh?

You howl/ Hear how you howl/ Tell me why you howl/ Tell me, no?/ Is it child?/ Did they take away your child?/ What have they done with your child/ That you knock your head with stone/ Bite your hand like dog-bone?

Or is it your husband you're crying for girl?/ What have they done to him/ That you daub your face with cow dung?/ Pierce your eyes and chop your tongue?/ Have they thrown him into the Demerara river, fed him to the alligators?

Is it your mother? Your father? Africa?/ Or are you pregnant by Massa?

You howl/ Hear how you howl/ Tell me how you howl/ Tell me, no?

COOLIE ODYSSEY

for Ma, d. 1985

Now that peasantry is in vogue,
Poetry bubbles from peat bogs,
People strain for the old folk's fatal gobs
Coughed up in grates North or North East
'Tween bouts o' living dialect,
It should be time to hymn your own wreck,
Your house the source of ancient song:
Dry coconut shells cackling in the fireside
Smoking up our children's eyes and lungs,
Plantains spitting oil from a clay pot,
Thick sugary black tea gulped down.

The calves hustle to suck,
Bawling on their rope but are beaten back
Until the cow is milked.
Frantic children call to be fed.
Roopram the Idiot goes to graze his father's goats backdam
Dreaming that the twig he chews so viciously in his mouth
Is not a twig.

In a winter of England's scorn
We huddle together memories, hoard them from
The opulence of our masters.

You were always back home, forever
As canefield and whiplash, unchanging
As the tombstones in the old Dutch plot
Which the boys used for wickets playing ball.

Over here Harilall who regularly dodged his duties at the
      marketstall
To spin bowl for us in the style of Ramadhin

And afterwards took his beatings from you heroically
In the style of England losing
Is now known as the local Paki
Doing slow trade in his Balham cornershop.
Is it because his heart is not in business
But in the tumble of wickets long ago
To the roar of wayward boys?
Or is it because he spends too much time
Being chirpy with his customers, greeting
The tight-wrapped pensioners stalking the snow
With tropical smile, jolly small chat, credit?
They like Harilall, these muted claws of Empire,
They feel privileged by his grinning service,
They hear steelband in his voice
And the freeness of the sea.
The sun beams from his teeth.

Heaped up beside you Old Dabydeen
Who on Albion Estate clean dawn
Washed obsessively by the canal bank,
Spread flowers on the snake-infested water,
Fed the gods the food that Chandra cooked,
Bathed his tongue of the creole
Babbled by low-caste infected coolies.
His Hindi chants terrorised the watertoads
Flopping to the protection of bush.
He called upon Lord Krishna to preserve
The virginity of his daughters
From the Negroes,
Prayed that the white man would honour
The end-of-season bonus to Poonai
The canecutter, his strong, only son:
Chandra's womb being cursed by deities
Like the blasted land
Unconquerable jungle or weed

71

That dragged the might of years from a man.
Chandra like a deaf-mute moved about the house
To his command,
A fearful bride barely come-of-age
Year upon year swelling with female child.
Guilt clenched her mouth
Smothered the cry of bursting apart:
Wrapped hurriedly in a bundle of midwife's cloth
The burden was removed to her mother's safekeeping.
He stamped and cursed and beat until he turned old
With the labour of chopping tree, minding cow, building
    fence
And the expense of his daughters' dowries.
Dreaming of India
He drank rum
Till he dropped dead
And was buried to the singing of Scottish Presbyterian
    hymns
And a hell-fire sermon from a pop-eyed bawling catechist,
By Poonai, lately baptised, like half the village.

Ever so old,
Dabydeen's wife,
Hobbling her way to fowl-pen,
Cussing low, chewing her cud, and lapsed in dream,
Sprinkling rice from her shrivelled hand.
Ever so old and bountiful,
Past where Dabydeen lazed in his mudgrave,
Idle as usual in the sun,
Who would dip his hand in a bowl of dhall and rice –
Nasty man, squelching and swallowing like a low-caste
    sow –
The bitch dead now!

The first boat chugged to the muddy port

Of King George's Town. Coolies come to rest
In El Dorado,
Their faces and best saris black with soot.
The men smelt of saltwater mixed with rum.
The odyssey was plank between river and land,
Mere yards but months of plotting
In the packed bowel of a white man's boat
The years of promise, years of expanse.

At first the gleam of the green land and the white folk and
     the Negroes,
The earth streaked with colour like a toucan's beak,
Kiskidees flame across a fortunate sky,
Canefields ripening in the sun
Wait to be gathered in armfuls of gold.

I have come back late and missed the funeral.
You will understand the connections were difficult.
Three airplanes boarded and many changes
Of machines and landscapes like reincarnations
To bring me to this library of graves,
This small clearing of scrubland.
There are no headstones, epitaphs, dates.
The ancestors curl and dry to scrolls of parchment.
They lie like texts
Waiting to be written by the children
For whom they hacked and ploughed and saved
To send to faraway schools.
Is foolishness fill your head.
Me dead.
Dog-bone and dry-well
Got no story to tell.
Just how me born stupid is so me gone.
Still we persist before the grave
Seeking fables.

73

We plunder for the maps of El Dorado
To make bountiful our minds in an England
Starved of gold.

Albion village sleeps, hacked
Out between bush and spiteful lip of river.
Folk that know bone
Fatten themselves on dreams
For the survival of days.
Mosquitoes sing at a nipple of blood.
A green-eyed moon watches
The rheumatic agony of houses crutched up on stilts
Pecked about by huge beaks of wind,
That bear the scars of ancient storms.
Crappeau clear their throats in hideous serenade,
Candleflies burst into suicidal flame.
In a green night with promise of rain
You die.

We mark your memory in songs
Fleshed in the emptiness of folk,
Poems that scrape bowl and bone
In English basements far from home,
Or confess the lust of beasts
In rare conceits
To congregations of the educated
Sipping wine, attentive between courses –
See the applause fluttering from their white hands
Like so many messy table napkins.